How to Write

An Awesome

Paragraph

Step-by-Step

Step-by-Step Study Skills

Happy Frog Writing Resources

Table of Contents

Introduction

Welcome to **How to Write an Awesome Paragraph Step-by-Step**.

This workbook teaches you how to write an excellent paragraph using a foolproof step-by-step process. Each incremental lesson teaches one step and contains practice examples to build your skill and confidence.

Part 1 introduces the parts of a paragraph.

In Part 2, you learn how to write an interesting topic sentence.

Part 3 guides you through adding relevant details.

Part 4 teaches you how write a closing sentence.

Part 5 helps you put it all together to write an amazing paragraph with interesting facts, relevant quotes and an effective ending.

In the Extras section, you'll find a handy, key-point summary and checklist, along with a link to an easily printable PDF version.

Get started right now and become a paragraph expert!

All About Paragraph Parts

A paragraph consists of a topic sentence, relevant details and a closing sentence. You'll learn about and practice each of these parts.

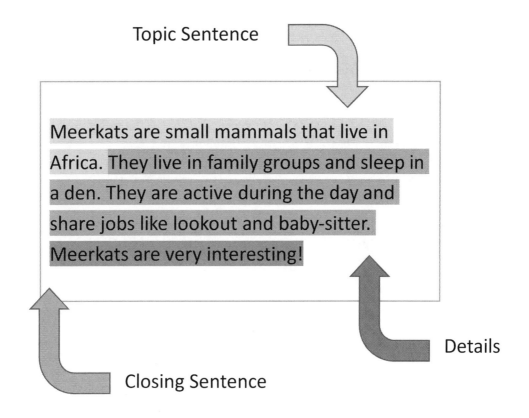

Topic Sentence

Meerkats are small mammals that live in Africa. They live in family groups and sleep in a den. They are active during the day and share jobs like lookout and baby-sitter. Meerkats are very interesting!

Details

Closing Sentence

Here's another example.

Topic Sentence

Morocco is a very interesting country in northern Africa. It has many beaches because it is next to the Atlantic Ocean and the Mediterranean Sea. If you like hiking, you can explore the Atlas mountains. If you like to study, Morocco has two main languages, Berber and Arabic. These are just some of the fascinating things about Morocco.

Details

Closing Sentence

All About
Topic Sentences

What is a Topic Sentence?

A topic sentence is a sentence that expresses the main idea of a paragraph. It tells what the entire paragraph will be about.

Topic Sentence

Camels like to be with other camels. In the wild, about thirty camels will walk around the desert together and look for food and water. Camels prefer not to fight with each other. They are happiest in herds.

Find the Topic Sentences 1

Underline or highlight the topic sentences in these paragraphs. Remember, a topic sentence expresses the main idea of the paragraph.

Zootopia is my favorite movie. I liked how Judy had a goal and worked towards it even when things became difficult. I also enjoyed many of the other characters. The music was excellent as well. I encourage everyone to watch this movie.

Japan is a fun place to visit. While I was there, I enjoyed trying many different foods. I also had fun visiting temples and shrines. The best part of all was riding the bullet train. It was an excellent vacation.

Australia has many unusual animals. One example is the kangaroo which can leap 9 meters in a single bound. Next is the echidna which has spines like a porcupine and a beak like a bird. Last, there is the platypus whose beak can detect electric signals. What a wonderful collection of strange animals!

Find the Topic Sentences 2

Underline or highlight the topic sentences in these paragraphs. Remember, a topic sentence expresses the main idea of the paragraph.

Kids should be careful about how much time they spend in front of a screen. Kids who watch more than two hours a day have lower scores on self-esteem. Also, more screen time is linked to higher obesity rates. Children should make good screen decisions so they stay healthy.

Regular exercise is very important. One reason to exercise regularly is to keep your bones strong. Another is to reduce your blood pressure. A third reason is to boost your energy. Start exercising today and enjoy better health.

Penguins are interesting birds. Unlike most birds, they lay their eggs on land and all nest together in a large group called a rookery. The father and mother take turns keeping the egg warm. When they are not on the nest, the parents swim in the ocean looking for food. There are many differences between penguins and other birds.

Decide the Topic 1

As a first step to writing topic sentences, let's identify the main idea or topic of these bullet points. The first one is done for you.

Topic: _____*Cats*_____

- Cat whiskers are the same length as their body.
- Cats sleep 12-16 hours per day.
- Grooming helps cats relax.

Topic: _____

- Snakes are carnivores.
- Snakes don't have eyelids.
- Snakes eat food whole.

Topic: _____

- China has more than 1 billion people.
- China is the 3rd largest country by area.
- 47% of the population of China live in urban areas.

Topic: _____

- The Great Wall of China is the longest man-made structure.
- The Great Wall is a UNESCO World Heritage site.
- The Great Wall is more than 2300 years old.

Decide the Topic 2

Identify the main idea or topic of these bullet points.

Topic: _____

- Eating a good breakfast boosts your energy levels.
- Eating a good breakfast leads to healthier choices in the rest of the day.
- Eating a good breakfast stimulates your brain.

Topic: _____

- Plan your homework before you start.
- Make sure you have all the books you need.
- Find a quiet place to work without distractions.

Topic: _____

- Pick up everything on the floor.
- Take out the trash.
- Sweep the floor.
- Put clothes and other things away.

Topic: _____

- The Eiffel Tower was completed in 1889.
- It was the tallest building until 1930.
- It has 1665 steps.

Choose the Best Topic Sentence 1

Select the best topic sentence from the box for each set of details.

Dogs are man's best friend.

Cooking requires a number of different skills.

Pavlova is my favorite dessert.

Vaccinations are important for pets.

Topic Sentence

_____

_____

- Cutting skills
- Measuring skills
- Following directions skills

Topic Sentence

_____

_____

- Make us feel better by wagging their tail.
- Support people with disabilities.
- Get us out walking which improves our health.

Choose the Best Topic Sentence 2

Select the best topic sentence from the box for each set of details.

> Dogs are man's best friend.
>
> Cooking requires a number of different skills.
>
> Pavlova is my favorite dessert.
>
> Vaccinations are important for pets.

Topic Sentence

_____

_____

- Prevents pets from getting some diseases.
- Prevents passing on diseases to owners.
- Can reduce problems like fleas.

Topic Sentence

_____

_____

- Easy to make.
- Light and fluffy to eat.
- Always have it for special occasions.

Create a Topic Sentence from a Prompt 1

Write a topic sentence based on the paragraph prompt. The first one is done for you.

Write about your favorite animal.

My favorite animal is the tiger. _____

Write about someone you care about and why they are important to you.

_____

If you could travel to the past, what would you do?

_____

Write about something you hope to do in the future.

_____

How much is the right amount of screen time for teenagers?

_____

Create a Topic Sentence from a Prompt 2

Write a topic sentence based on the prompt.

Write about a dream you have had.

_____

Write about your favorite movie.

_____

Write about someone you admire.

_____

Should schools have uniforms?

_____

Write about your favorite hobby.

_____

Write a Topic Sentence from Paragraph Details 1

Write a topic sentence based on the list of details.

Topic Sentence:

_____

- You can eat more healthily when you cook at home.
- You can save money by eating at home.
- You can make dishes at home that you can't buy locally.

Topic Sentence:

_____

- Graduating high school means you can go to college.
- Graduating high school gives you more job options.
- Graduating high school leads to higher wages.

Write a Topic Sentence from Paragraph Details 2

Write a topic sentence based on the list of details.

Topic Sentence:

_____

- A driving instructor can teach safe driving habits straight away.
- Your parents won't get frustrated trying to teach you how to drive.
- Using a driving instructor means you might get a discount on your car insurance.
- When you learn from a driving instructor, you learn from someone who is a professional at teaching how to drive.

Topic Sentence:

_____

- Organize your study space.
- Make a list of things you need to study.
- Plan out your study schedule.
- Remove distractions while you work.

Write a Topic Sentence 1

Write a topic sentence to go with each paragraph.

Topic Sentence:

_____

First we lit our lamps, and then we went into the cave. It was very dark inside and I was a little scared. Surprisingly, I got used to it quite quickly and I was disappointed when we had to leave. Ape Cave was an exciting experience!

Topic Sentence:

_____

The first animal they saw was a lion. It was very big with a fluffy mane around its neck. Next, they went to look at the monkeys. The monkeys were very active and swung from branches and jumped over rocks. After that they were hungry so John's dad bought them burgers. It was another great day at the zoo.

Topic Sentence:

_____

We both have black hair and brown eyes. We are both tall and skinny. We both love playing Minecraft all the time! Having a twin is great.

Write a Topic Sentence 2

Write a topic sentence to go with each paragraph.

Topic Sentence:

_____

The Allure of the Seas is 1,187 feet long. She is 213 feet wide. She weighs more than 225 thousand tons. There are many activities for passengers. I would love to go on this boat.

Topic Sentence:

_____

Astronauts live on the space station for weeks or months. They do science experiments to learn more about living in space. Being an astronaut on the space station is a fascinating job.

Topic Sentence:

_____

It was built in 1889 using 18 thousand pieces of iron and more than 2 million rivets. It is over 300 feet tall. More than 6 million people visit the Eiffel Tower every year. What an amazing monument!

Advanced Topic Sentences

Topic sentences are not always the first sentence in a paragraph. See if you can identify the topic sentences in these paragraphs. Remember, the topic sentence tells you what details you will find in the rest of the paragraph.

Pavlova is a creamy, crunchy, delicious dessert. Here's how you make it. First whip eggs whites. Next add sugar and vanilla. Bake it in a hot oven and garnish it with whipped cream and fruit. I am sure you will enjoy this scrumptious dish.

For many months, I couldn't see the board at school. Then, last month, my mom took me to an eye doctor and my problem was solved. It turns out I was short-sighted, and I needed glasses. Once I got my glasses, I could see everything. I was amazed. If you have trouble seeing things, get your eyesight checked.

When a camera flash is used, the subject's eyes can appear red in the finished photograph. This problem can be reduced by using the red-eye feature found in many cameras. This feature activates a quick flash directly before the regular flash. The pupils in the subject's eyes will close and this means less chance of the red-eye occurring. Use the red-eye feature on your camera to reduce this problem.

Upgrading Your Topic Sentence

If you feel like your topic sentences need more variety, there are several strategies you can use.

Here are five quick ways to add interest to your topic sentences.

- Ask a **question**
- Introduce a **comparison**
- State an **interesting fact**
- Set the scene with **a description.**
- Encourage **shock/excitement**

Let's try each with the same base paragraph.

Question:
Did you know camels are quite social? It's true. Camels like to be with other camels. In the wild, about thirty camels will walk around the desert together and look for food and water. Camels prefer not to fight with each other. They are happiest in herds.

Comparison:
Camels are the dogs of the desert. Like dogs, camels are friendly and like to be with members of their species. In the wild, about thirty camels will walk around the desert together and look for food and water. Camels prefer not to fight with each other. They are happiest in herds.

Fact:

Although camels can weigh over 400 kg, they are friendly, social animals. In particular, camels like to be with other camels. In the wild about thirty camels will walk around the desert together and look for food and water. Camels prefer not to fight with each other. They are happiest in herds.

Note: Your interesting fact should be a specific statistic (like a number), rather than vague words like 'a lot', etc.

Description:

Across the shimmering dry desert sand, a group of camels graze. This is not unusual as camels like to be with other camels. In the wild about thirty camels will walk around the desert together and look for food and water. Camels prefer not to fight with each other. They are happiest in herds.

Note: Some learners find the description upgrade to be very challenging. We've included additional lessons on description upgrades in the Extras section at the end of the book.

Shock/Excitement:

Big news! Although camels come across as solitary creatures, in fact, camels like to be with other camels. In the wild about thirty camels will walk around the desert together and look for food and water. Camels prefer not to fight with each other. They are happiest in herds.

Use these strategies to upgrade your topic sentences.

Upgrade Your Topic Sentence 1

Now it's your turn to practice. Rewrite the underlined topic sentence to upgrade it.

<u>Meerkats are small mammals that live in Africa</u>. They live in family groups and sleep in a den. They are active during the day and share jobs like lookout and baby-sitter. Meerkats are very interesting!

Question:_____

_____

Comparison:_____

_____

Fact:_____

_____

Description:_____

_____

Excitement:_____

_____

Upgrade Your Topic Sentence 2

Now it's your turn to practice. Rewrite the underlined topic sentence to upgrade it.

Japan is a fun place to visit. While I was there, I enjoyed trying many different foods. I also had fun visiting temples and shrines. The best part of all was riding the bullet train. It was an excellent vacation.

Question:_____

_____

Comparison:_____

_____

Fact:_____

_____

Description:_____

_____

Excitement:_____

_____

Topic Sentences Summary

A topic sentence is a sentence that **expresses the main idea** of a paragraph. It tells what the entire paragraph will be about.

The topic sentence **is often the first sentence** in the paragraph, but sometimes the paragraph starts off with some upgrades.

You can **upgrade your topic sentence** using any of these strategies.

- Ask a **question**
- Introduce a **comparison**
- State an **interesting fact**
- Set the scene with **a description.**
- Encourage **shock/excitement**

Time to Write 1

You've learned about topic sentences, so let's write a paragraph. You've still got lots to learn about the other parts of the paragraph, but let's write anyway!

Choose one of the topics.

Topic 1: Describe a place you would like to visit. Explain why.

Or

Topic 2: Write about a famous explorer.

_____

_____

_____

_____

_____

_____

_____

_____

_____

Don't forget to upgrade your topic sentence!

All About
Relevant Details

What are Relevant Details?

Relevant details give information about the paragraph topic. These are facts, quotes or personal experiences that support or give evidence for the topic sentence.

Camels like to be with other camels. In the wild, about thirty camels will walk around the desert together and look for food and water. Camels prefer not to fight with each other. They are happiest in herds.

Details

Identify the Relevant Details

Underline or highlight the relevant details in these paragraphs. Remember, relevant details add information about the main idea of the paragraph.

Penguins are interesting birds. Unlike most birds, they lay their eggs on land and all nest together in a large group called a rookery. The father and mother take turns keeping the egg warm. When they are not on the nest, they swim in the ocean looking for food. There are many differences between penguins and other birds.

The Appalachians are the longest group of mountains in eastern North America. These mountains start in the northern U.S. state of Maine. They end in the southern state of Georgia. The Appalachian Trail through the mountains is about 2,200 miles long. The Appalachians would be a great place to visit.

Allergies are an unusual feature of the human body. An allergy occurs when the body's immune system sees a substance as harmful and overreacts to it. The substances that cause allergic reactions are allergens. Allergies are one of the most common chronic diseases. I hope you don't have allergies!

Sort the Relevant Details 1

Under each topic sentence, list the relevant details for that topic sentence. Not all the details will be used.

Topic Sentence 1:
Have you heard about the Oregon Trail? It's an historic wagon route.

Topic Sentence 2:
Worms are very interesting creatures.

_____

_____

A. Instead they breathe through their skin.

B. The trail passed through what is now Kansas, Nebraska, Wyoming, Idaho and Oregon.

C. The Oregon Trail was 2,170-mile long and connected the Missouri River to valleys in Oregon.

D. They do not have lungs or other breathing organs.

E. The tower is 600 meters high.

F. Their skin also produces a fluid that makes moving through underground burrows easier.

Sort the Relevant Details 2

Under each topic sentence, list the relevant details for that topic sentence. Not all the details will be used.

Topic Sentence 1:
Space junk is any piece of machinery or rubbish left by humans in space.

_____

Topic Sentence 2:
More people should know about Mercury.

_____

A. Space junk may be big, like a dead satellite.

B. The planet orbits the sun in only 88 Earth days, faster than any other planet in our solar system.

C. Mercury is the smallest planet in our solar system and the closest to the sun.

D. They do not have lungs or other breathing organs.

E. Or it can be tiny, like small paint flecks.

Which One Doesn't Belong?

Each of your relevant details needs to support the topic sentence. Below, practice identifying which detail does not directly support the topic sentence.

Keep in mind, the detail might be related to the topic, but to be a relevant detail, it must prove the topic sentence or give examples that support the topic sentence.

We can take steps to minimize wasting water.

- Take shorter showers.
- Turn off water while brushing your teeth.
- Reducing water usage is good for the planet.

All schools should have uniforms.

- Uniforms encourage a sense of community.
- Australian schools have uniforms.
- A common uniform reduces bullying based on clothing choices.

Add Relevant Details 1

Add three relevant details for each topic sentence.

Today Dana had the best day ever.

- _____
- _____
- _____

Let me tell you why _____ is my favorite movie.

- _____
- _____
- _____

Cats are better than dogs.

- _____
- _____
- _____

Add Relevant Details 2

Add three relevant details for each topic sentence.

My family has several traditions at Christmas.

- _____
- _____
- _____

Winter is the best season because of all the fun activities.

- _____
- _____
- _____

Schools should have longer holidays.

- _____
- _____
- _____

Add Relevant Details 3

Sometimes you might need to do research in order to find relevant details. Add three relevant details for each topic sentence below. Ask your teacher whether you should use books or the internet.

Marco Polo was an intrepid explorer.

- _____

- _____

- _____

Australia has many unusual animals.

- _____

- _____

- _____

Secondary colors are made by mixing primary colors.

- _____

- _____

- _____

Add Relevant Details 4

Sometimes you might need to do research in order to find relevant details. Add three relevant details for each topic sentence below. Ask your teacher whether you should use books or the internet.

Water can exist in three forms.

- _____
- _____
- _____

Some countries celebrate Christmas in different ways.

- _____
- _____
- _____

The northern lights are an amazing natural phenomenon.

- _____
- _____
- _____

Write Relevant Details 1

Add three relevant details for the topic sentence. Next, write the whole paragraph. You haven't learned about closing sentences yet, so don't worry too much about that.

Topic sentence: We should protect endangered animals.

- _____

- _____

- _____

_____

_____

_____

_____

_____

_____

_____

Write Relevant Details 2

Add three relevant details for the topic sentence. Next, write the whole paragraph. You haven't learned about closing sentences yet, so don't worry too much about that.

Topic sentence: A good friend has these three characteristics.

- _____
- _____
- _____

_____

_____

_____

_____

_____

_____

_____

_____

Write Relevant Details 3

Add three relevant details for the topic sentence. Next, write the whole paragraph. You haven't learned about closing sentences yet, so don't worry too much about that.

Topic sentence: Growing a garden is good for many reasons.

- _____
- _____
- _____

_____

_____

_____

_____

_____

_____

_____

Write Relevant Details 4

Add three relevant details for the topic sentence. Next, write the whole paragraph. You haven't learned about closing sentences yet, so don't worry too much about that.

Topic sentence: Remember these three things to have a good day at school.

- _____
- _____
- _____

_____

_____

_____

_____

_____

_____

_____

_____

Upgrade Your Relevant Details

There are several ways to upgrade the quality of your relevant details.

You can:

- Add **transition words**
- Include **specific facts**
- Include direct or indirect **quotes**
- Remove **weak words & repeated phrases**

Transition example:

Instead of: You add milk. You add eggs.

Add transitions: **First,** you add milk. **Next,** you add eggs.

Specific Facts example:

Instead of: The tower was tall.

You add specific data: The tower was **600 feet** tall.

Direct and indirect quotes example:

Instead of: The virus spreads easily.

Use an indirect quote:

According to Science News Daily, the virus spreads easily.

Use a direct quote:

Dr John Smith states, "The virus spreads easily."

Weak words & repeated phrases example:

Instead of: I plan to get a job and then get a house.

Add stronger words: I plan to **obtain** a job and then **buy** a house.

You'll learn and practice how to do each of these in the following pages.

Relevant Details Upgrade # 1
Transition Words

Transition words give signposts to the reader about where you are going next.

For example, saying "first", lets your reader know you will be giving several pieces of information, or will be telling them several steps. When you say "second" or "next", you let your reader know they are getting the second piece of information.

Another example is the transition word "However." This lets the reader know that you may be about to say something opposite to what they might expect.

For example: I like ice cream. However, pie is my favorite dessert.

On the opposite page, you will find a table of some easy-to-use transition words. Next, you'll practice using them.

List of Transition Words

Beginning	First, To begin with, In the beginning, One example
Continue	Next, Also, After that, To continue, In addition, Furthermore, Another reason, Another example, Eventually
Alike	Similarly, Along the same lines, In comparison, Additionally, Likewise
Different	However, Although, On the other hand, In contrast
Result	As a result, Consequently, For these reasons, Therefore
Time	Suddenly, Occasionally, Frequently, When, Until
Example	For example, For instance, To illustrate
Quote	As X says, According to X, X states
Finish	In conclusion, In summary, Last, Finally, In the end, To sum up, In short

Find the Transition Words

Underline all the transitions in these paragraphs.

There are over 100 buildings in the world more than one thousand feet tall. However, the tallest building is the Burj Khalifa. The Burj Khalifa is amazing for several reasons.

First, this building is 2,722 feet tall, almost 1 kilometer! Can you imagine how tall that is?

Second, the Burj Khalifa cost $1.5 billion dollars to build. Construction of the Burj Khalifa started in 2004 and finished in 2009.

The Burj Khalifa building is in Dubai. Although most people think Dubai is a country, it is not. In fact, it is one of the seven Emirates in the United Arab Emirates.

Even the name of the building is interesting. Burj means tower in Arabic. Khalifa is the name of the leader of the United Arab Emirates.

The Burj Khalifa has won many awards. It has broken records for the highest restaurant and the highest swimming pool. In addition, it has the highest observation deck in the world.

To sum up, the Burj Khalifa is truly amazing!

Practice Transitions 1

Practice using the transitions by making up a sentence to go with each of the listed transitions.

For example, _____

_____

In addition, _____

_____

To begin with, _____

_____

In conclusion, _____

_____

However, _____

_____

Practice Transitions 2

Practice using the transitions by making up a sentence to go with each
of the listed transitions.

Next, _____

_____

Similarly, _____

_____

Although, _____

_____

As mom says, _____

_____

Frequently, _____

_____

Choose the Transition 1

Choose the correct transition from the choices available.

_____ Sam was sick, his mother made him stay home.

1. Because   2. In addition   3. Only

_____ , these are the reasons why I believe we should get longer lunch breaks.

1. Because   2. In conclusion   3. Frequently

Georgia likes math. _____ , her favorite subject is art.

1. First   2. Although   3. However

I cleaned my room, did my homework and walked the dog. _____ , I should be allowed to do screen time.

1. Only   2. As a result   3. However

Choose the Transition 2

Choose the correct transition from the choices available.

_____ , put in the flour. _____ , add the eggs.

1. Next   2. First   3. In addition

_____ , rain poured out of the sky and we all got wet.

1. In addition   2. In conclusion   3. Suddenly

_____ , one way to prepare eggs is to fry them.

1. For example   2. Frequently   3. Only

_____ , like cats, dogs also have four legs.

1. Only   2. Sometimes   3. Similarly

Insert Transitions 1

Complete these paragraphs by inserting transitions.

Today, lots of cars are fast. _____, the fastest car of all is called the Bugatti Veyron Super Sport.

_____, the Bugatti Veyron Super Sport can go up to 268 miles per hour! If you drive at top speed, the tires will wear out in 15 minutes.

It is also very expensive. _____, the car costs more than a million dollars to buy. If you need to replace the tires, it will cost you $42,000.

_____, the Super Sport is a really fantastic car.

Insert Transitions 2

Complete these paragraphs by inserting transitions.

Many dangerous animals are big. They have sharp teeth and sharp claws. _____, the most dangerous animal in the world is actually quite small. It is called the box jellyfish. Here are several interesting facts about this fish.

_____, Box jellyfish live mostly in the ocean near Australia. They are pale blue and are transparent in color and get their name from the cube-like shape of their bell.

_____, up to 15 tentacles grow from each corner of the bell and can be up to 10 feet long. Each tentacle has about 5 thousand stinging cells. _____, these stingers are not triggered by touch. _____, they are triggered by chemicals on the skin of its prey.

_____, the venom from the box jellyfish can kill a human in 2 to 5 minutes.

_____, this sounds like a really interesting animal... but I sure don't want to meet one!

Relevant Details Upgrade # 2
Specific Facts

Another way to upgrade your relevant details is to include specific facts.

Instead of saying a cruise ship is "big", research the specific details and instead state, "The Allure of the Seas is 1167 feet long."

You will need to seek information in books or the internet to upgrade your paragraph with specific details.

Let's practice adding specific facts.

Find the Specific Facts

Identify the specific facts in the upgraded paragraphs.

Original:

Box jelly fish have many long tentacles. Each tentacle has many stinging cells. Interestingly, these stingers are not triggered by touch. Instead, they are triggered by chemicals on the skin of its prey.

Upgraded:

Box jelly fish have many tentacles. Up to 15 tentacles grow from each corner of the bell and they can be up to 10 feet long. Each tentacle has about 5 thousand stinging cells. Interestingly, these stingers are not triggered by touch. Instead, they are triggered by chemicals on the skin of its prey.

Original:

Do you know about Bullet trains? Bullet trains are very fast, long distance trains in Japan. They also carry lots of passengers. I hope to travel on one of these amazing trains one day.

Upgraded:

Do you know about Bullet trains? Bullet trains are very fast, long distance trains in Japan. Amazingly, these trains travel at 320km/h. That's 200mph. Each train can carry over 1000 passengers. I hope to travel on one of these amazing trains one day.

Add Specific Facts 1

Rewrite these details to include some specific facts.

Original:

Today was really hot.

Upgraded:_____

_____

_____

_____

Original:

The world's oldest living land creature is a giant tortoise that lives in Africa. It's really old.

Upgraded:_____

_____

_____

_____

Add Specific Facts 2

Rewrite these details to include some specific facts.

Original:

The largest cruise ship in the world is very big and can carry many passengers. The passengers have lots of different places to eat on this boat.

Upgraded:_____

_____

_____

_____

Original:

The ocean can get really deep. Some animals live really deep in the ocean. Humans have gone quite deep, but not as deep as some animals.

Upgraded:_____

_____

_____

_____

Relevant Details Upgrade # 3
Direct & Indirect Quotes

Another way to upgrade your relevant details is to include quotes.

Quotes can be **direct**, when you are repeating the exact words someone used, or **indirect**, when you paraphrase what someone said.

Direct quotes use quotation marks " ". Indirect quotes do not use quotation marks.

All quotes should be attributed, or linked, to the original author.

Here are some examples.

Direct Quotes:
- Marie Antoinette said, "Let them eat cake."
- I was ready to go out, but then I heard my mom say, "Clean your room or else."
- Vet Peter Andrews stated, "The dog was most likely poisoned by a deadly snake."

Indirect Quotes:
- My mom told me to clean my room.
- Marie Antoinette told people to eat cake.
- According to vet Peter Andrews, the dog was poisoned by a deadly snake.

Write Direct & Indirect Quotes

Write a direct quote and an indirect quote based on the article excerpt.

Joshua Bedford believes he saw a fairy in his garden. "It was right over there," he said, pointing towards his garage.

Direct Quote: _____

_____

Indirect Quote: _____

_____

Dave Ramsay is quoted as saying, "We live in a culture full of hares, but the tortoise always wins."

Direct Quote: _____

_____

Indirect Quote: _____

_____

Integrate a Quote Into a Paragraph

Write a paragraph based on these bullet points. Make sure to use a direct or indirect quote.

Topic Sentence: There are many reasons why graduating high school is a good idea.

- Graduating high school means you can go to college.
- Graduating high school gives you more job options.
- Principal Mary Martin says, "Graduating high school is the first step to a successful life."
- Graduating high school leads to higher wages.

_____

_____

_____

_____

_____

_____

_____

_____

Relevant Details Upgrade # 4
Remove Weak/Repeated Words

Removing weak words or repeated phrases is a great way to improve the quality of your paragraph.

Weak words are vague words that should be replaced with stronger, more specific words – or sometimes just deleted. The top weak words to look out for are:

Thing	It, There (not always weak.)
Just	Very, Really
Get/Got	Good, Nice, Bad
I think, I believe	

Instead of: The best **thing** about school is recess.

Try: School's best feature is recess.

Instead of: **I just believe** red is the **very** best color.

Try: Red is the best color.

Repeated phrases are phrases that you use too often within a paragraph. Rewrite the sentence to avoid the repetition.

In summary, these are the reasons why I choose to work **in a furniture shop**. I hope I will work in **a furniture shop** one day.

In summary, these are the reasons why I choose to work **in a furniture shop**. I hope I obtain this dream job one day.

Identify Weak Words & Repeated Phrases

Identify the weak words and repeated phrases in these paragraphs.

Find 3 weak words and one repeated phrase.

Box jelly fish have got many really long tentacles. Each tentacle has many stinging cells. Interestingly, these crazy stingers are not triggered by touch. Instead, these crazy stingers are just triggered by chemicals on the skin of its prey.

Find at least 3 weak words and one repeated phrase. (One weak word isn't in the list.)

The Hoover Dam is a really big concrete dam that blocks the Colorado River on the border between Nevada and Arizona in the U.S. It got finished in 1936 and was the largest dam in the world at that time. The lake behind it is called Lake Mead. The dam and Lake Mead are super popular tourist destinations. If you like super popular tourist destinations, you should just plan to visit one day. Do you think you will?

Fix Weak/Repeated Words

Rewrite the paragraph to remove the underlined weak words and repeated phrases.

My favorite flower is the daffodil. I like the daffodil because it is a really nice and happy color. I also like it because it blooms in spring after the long winter. I get daffodils on my birthday every year. I think daffodils will always be my favorite flower.

_____

_____

_____

_____

_____

Cats should be kept inside for several very good reasons. First, depending on where you live, you may get really good predators such as coyotes that will attack it. Second, cats are really good predators, too, and can really decimate the songbird population really quickly. Although cats like get outside, they should be kept inside for the safety of all animals.

_____

_____

_____

_____

_____

Relevant Details Summary

Relevant details give information about the paragraph topic. These are facts, quotes or personal experiences that support the topic sentence.

Most paragraphs should have 2-5 relevant details.

You can **upgrade your relevant details** by using any of these strategies.

- Add **transition words**
- Introduce **specific facts**
- Add a **direct or indirect quote**
- Remove **weak words & repeated phrases**

Time to Write 2

You've learned about topic sentences **and** relevant details, so let's rewrite the paragraph you wrote earlier.

Feel free to refer back to your original version.

Topic 1: Describe a place you would like to visit. Explain why.

Or

Topic 2: Write about a famous explorer.

_____

_____

_____

_____

_____

_____

_____

_____

Don't forget to upgrade your relevant details.

All About the Closing Sentence

What is a Closing Sentence?

The closing sentence summarizes the main idea of the paragraph. It does not add any new details.

The closing sentence can say the same thing as the topic sentence, but it should use different words.

Camels like to be with other camels. In the wild, about thirty camels will walk around the desert together and look for food and water. Camels prefer not to fight with each other. They are happiest in herds.

Closing Sentence

Identify the Closing Sentence

Highlight or underline the closing sentences in these paragraphs.

The world's tallest sandcastle was nearly 58 feet high. It was built in Germany in 2019 for a competition. An international team of 12 sculptors and eight technicians from Russia, Poland, Hungary, Germany, Holland and Latvia created the huge structure in three-and-a-half weeks. What an amazing feat!

Do you know about matter? Everything around us is made of matter—your hair, plants, even the air you breathe! There are four states of matter: liquid, gas, solid, and plasma. Water is an example of a liquid. Steam is an example of a gas. Ice is an example of a solid. The sun is an example of plasma. In sum, matter matters.

The Hoover Dam is a concrete dam that blocks the Colorado River on the border between Nevada and Arizona in the U.S. It was finished in 1936 and was the largest dam in the world at that time. The lake behind it is called Lake Mead. The dam and Lake Mead are popular tourist destinations. You should plan to visit one day. Do you think you will?

Choose a Closing Sentence

Write the appropriate closing sentence under each paragraph.

Most people think deserts are hot, but both hot and cold deserts exist.

No matter what their shape, donuts taste good!

I think being an astronaut would be a fascinating job.

An astronaut is a person who goes into space. The first person in space was from Russia. His name was Yuri Gagarin. This happened on April 12, 1961. The first person to walk on the moon was from America. His name was Neil Armstrong. He walked on the moon on July 20, 1969. _____

_____

There are both hot and cold deserts in the world. The largest hot desert is the Sahara. It is in northern Africa. It is nearly as large as the whole United States. The largest cold desert is Antarctica. Antarctica is the coldest place on Earth._____

_____

There are 3 types of donuts. Ring donuts are shaped like a ring. Filled donuts are round. They have jam, cream or chocolate inside. There are also donut "holes". These are shaped like a small ball.

_____

_____

Add a Closing Sentence 1

Add a closing sentence to each paragraph.

Carlsbad Caverns National Park is a national park in New Mexico. Carlsbad Caverns is one of the oldest and most famous cave systems in the world. The caverns include several vast underground chambers, up to 250 feet high, filled with amazing formations of many colors and shapes. _____

_____

Singapore is an island country in Southeast Asia. It is quite near the equator. The country is home to 5.7 million people. There are four official languages: English, Malay, Chinese and Tamil. Singapore's culture, food and festivals are very diverse because of its rich cultural history. _____

_____

Tokyo Sky Tree is a 634 meter tall tower in Tokyo, Japan. It is the tallest tower in the world. The Sky Tree has a great view of Tokyo and sometimes Mt Fuji is visible as well. There are lots of windows for viewing and even a see-through floor that you can stand on. _____

_____

Add a Closing Sentence 2

Add a closing sentence to each paragraph

The Lion dance is a traditional dance in several Asian cultures. During the dance, performers mimic a lion's movements while wearing a lion costume. The dance is done to bring good luck and fortune. The lion dance is usually performed during the Chinese New Year and other important occasions. _____
_____ _____

Chopsticks are eating utensils that were first used in the 3rd century. They can be made of metal or wood. When using wooden chopsticks, rub one chopstick against the other before you eat. This makes the chopsticks nice and smooth. _____
_____

The piano is a musical instrument invented in Italy around the year 1700. It is played using a keyboard of back and white keys. The piano was different from previous, similar instruments because it could be played loudly or softly. _____
_____

Upgrade Your Closing Sentences

You can improve your closing sentences by using the following techniques to add variety.

Add Transitions

Don't forget you can use transitions like "In conclusion," "In summary."

Add a Future Thought

To conclude, camels are very social animals. I hope that humans can be more like camels.

Add Encouragement to Action

In sum, camels are very social animals. We should all be as friendly!

Add a Question about the Content

As you can see camels are very social animals. Are you as social as a camel?

Add a Personal Opinion

Camels are very social animals. I think they are quite interesting.

Upgrade Your Closing Sentence 1

Add to or rewrite the closing sentence to include the specified upgrades.

Do you know about Bullet trains? Bullet trains are very fast, long distance trains in Japan. Amazingly, these trains travel at 320km/h. That's 200mph. The trains also carry over a thousand passengers. **These are amazing trains**.

Add a transition: _____

_____

Add a future thought: _____

_____

Add encouragement to action: _____

_____

Add a question about the content: _____

_____

Add a personal opinion: _____

_____

Upgrade Your Closing Sentence 2

Add to or rewrite the closing sentence to include the specified extra upgrade.

Penguins are interesting birds. Unlike most birds, they lay their eggs on land and all nest together in a large group called a rookery. The father and mother take turns keeping the egg warm. When they are not on the nest, they swim in the ocean looking for food. **There are many differences between penguins and other birds.**

Add a transition: _____

_____

Add a future thought: _____

_____

Add encouragement to action: _____

_____

Add a question about the content: _____

_____

Add a personal opinion: _____

_____

Closing Sentence Summary

The closing sentence summarizes the main idea of the paragraph. It does not add any new details.

The closing sentence can say the same thing as the topic sentence, but it should use different words.

You can improve your closing sentences by using the following techniques to add variety.

- Adding **transition words**
- Introducing a **future thought**
- Adding an **encouragement to action**
- Including a **question about the content**
- Adding a **personal opinion**

Time to Write 3

You've learned about topic sentences, relevant details and closing sentences, so let's rewrite that paragraph again.

Feel free to refer back to your last version.

Topic 1: Describe a place you would like to visit. Explain why.

Or

Topic 2: Write about a famous explorer.

_____

_____

_____

_____

_____

_____

_____

_____

Don't forget to upgrade your closing sentence.

Putting It All Together Writing Complete Paragraphs

You have learned a lot about the different parts of a paragraph.

Now let's put your skills to work in creating some wonderful writing.

Below is a handy checklist for checking your writing when you are done. And on the next page, we include a summary of the key points you have learned.

Paragraph Checklist

- ❑ Topic sentence
- ❑ 2-5 relevant details
- ❑ Closing sentence
- ❑ One or more transitions
- ❑ One or more other upgrades
- ❑ Spelling checked
- ❑ Grammar checked

Writing a Paragraph: Key Points

A topic sentence is a sentence that expresses the main idea of a paragraph. It tells what the entire paragraph will be about.	**Topic sentence** upgrades: • Ask a **question** • Introduce a **comparison** • State an **interesting fact** • Set the scene with **a description.** • Encourage **shock/excitement**
Relevant details give information about the paragraph topic. These are facts, quotes or personal experiences that support the topic sentence.	**Relevant details** upgrades: • Add **transition words** • Introduce **specific facts** • Add a **direct or indirect quote** • Fix **weak words & repeated phrases**
The **closing sentence** summarizes the main idea of the paragraph. It does not add any new details.	**Closing sentence** upgrades: • Add **transition words** • Introduce a **future thought** • Add an **encouragement to action** • Include a **question about the content** • Add a **personal opinion**

Write a Paragraph 1

Now it's your turn to write a complete paragraph. Use the bullet points to outline your ideas if you wish.

Describe how to make a sandwich.

Topic Sentence:_____

- • _____

- • _____

- • _____

Conclusion: _____

_____

_____

_____

_____

_____

_____

_____

_____

Write a Paragraph 2

Now it's your turn to write a complete paragraph. Use the bullet points to outline your ideas if you wish.

If you could travel into the future, what would you do?

Topic Sentence:_____

- • _____
- • _____
- • _____

Conclusion: _____

_____

_____

_____

_____

_____

_____

_____

_____

_____

Write a Paragraph 3

Now it's your turn to write a complete paragraph. Use the bullet points to outline your ideas if you wish.

What does friendship mean to you?

Topic Sentence:_____

- _____

- _____

- _____

Conclusion: _____

_____

_____

_____

_____

_____

_____

_____

_____

_____

Write a Paragraph 4

Now it's your turn to write a complete paragraph. Use the bullet points to outline your ideas if you wish.

Describe how our lives would be different if the computer was never invented.

Topic Sentence:_____

- •   _____
- •   _____
- •   _____

Conclusion: _____

_____

_____

_____

_____

_____

_____

_____

_____

Write a Paragraph 5

Now it's your turn to write a complete paragraph. Use the bullet points to outline your ideas if you wish.

Should we colonize Mars? Explain why or why not.

Topic Sentence:_____

- _____

- _____

- _____

Conclusion: _____

_____

_____

_____

_____

_____

_____

_____

_____

Write a Paragraph 6

Now it's your turn to write a complete paragraph. Use the bullet points to outline your ideas if you wish.

Is social media good or bad?

Topic Sentence:_____

- • _____
- • _____
- • _____

Conclusion: _____

_____

_____

_____

_____

_____

_____

_____

_____

Extras

Our Extras section contains additional information to support your paragraph writing development. Here you will find:

1.   An additional upgrade for relevant details. This upgrade is useful for when you write essays.

2.   More practice for upgrading your topic sentence with descriptions.

3.   An updated copy of the Paragraph Writing Key Points that includes the extra upgrade.

4.   A copy of the paragraph checklist.

The Key Points and checklist can be downloaded at:

https://happyfroglearning.com/product/paragraph-pdf/

Getting Ready to Write Essays

The paragraph skills you have built are just what you need to write excellent essays. However, if you are ready to start writing essays, there is one more upgrade you should learn about.

Relevant Details Upgrade #5 Supporting Details

The supporting details upgrade is somewhat like a combination of upgrade #2, specific facts, and #3, direct or indirect quotes.

Supporting details are details from a reference text that support the topic sentence. When you extract supporting details, you should paraphrase them in your own words and reference the source of the information.

Here's an example.

Super Science News

Saturn Losing Its Rings

Scientists from NASA have confirmed that Saturn is losing its rings. The iconic rings are being pulled into the planet by gravity.

Essay Excerpt

Another example of recent changes in space is the movement in Saturn's rings. According to Super Science News, the rings are being sucked in by the planet's gravity.

If you are ready for essays, download practice pages for this upgrade from our website: https://geni.us/extrapages/

Topic Sentence: Description Upgrade Practice

Earlier in the book you learned about upgrading your topic sentence by using descriptions. Here are some extra tips for creating a great description upgrade.

To create a good description, **first think of the five senses** and how they relate to the topic sentence. Also think about the feelings you get when you think about the topic sentence.

For example, here are some brainstormed/researched ideas for two topic sentences.

	Japan is a fun place to visit	Meerkats are small mammals that live in Africa.
Sounds	Temple bells, whoosh of bullet train, slurping noodles	squealing and chattering
Feelings	Serene temples	?
Smells	Incense at temples	>
Sight	Tall buildings	Stand tall as a lookout
Touch	?	soft smooth fur
Taste	Unusual tastes	?

Topic Sentence: Description Upgrade Practice

Once you have brainstormed some sensory phrases, **choose one or two and create a sentence or phrase that connects to your topic sentence.**

For example:

With the whoosh of a bullet train and the serenity of a peaceful temple, Japan is a fun place to visit.

The smell of incense hangs in the air as the temple comes into view. For so many reasons, Japan is a fun place to visit.

The sound of slurping noodles reminds me of Japan and what a fun place it is to visit.

While their soft, smooth fur makes them seem like cute pets, Meerkats are small wild mammals that live in Africa.

Chattering and squealing shows the presence of meerkats, a small wild mammal that lives in Africa.

Topic Sentence:
Description Practice 1

Brainstorm some sensory details for this topic sentence. Next, upgrade the topic sentence with a description upgrade.

Growing a garden is good for many reasons.

Sounds	
Feelings	
Smells	
Sight	
Touch	
Taste	

_____

_____

_____

_____

Topic Sentence:
Description Practice 2

Brainstorm some sensory details for this topic sentence. Next, upgrade the topic sentence with a description upgrade.

The Burj Khalifa is the tallest building in the world.

Sounds	
Feelings	
Smells	
Sight	
Touch	
Taste	

_____

_____

_____

_____

Writing a Paragraph: Key Points

A topic sentence is a sentence that expresses the main idea of a paragraph. It tells what the entire paragraph will be about.	**Topic sentence** upgrades: • Ask a **question** • Introduce a **comparison** • State an **interesting fact** • Set the scene with **a description.** • Encourage **shock/excitement**
Relevant details give information about the paragraph topic. These are facts, quotes or personal experiences that support the topic sentence.	**Relevant details** upgrades: • Add **transition words** • Introduce **specific facts** • Add a **direct or indirect quote** • Fix **weak words & repeated phrases** • Reference **supporting details**
The **closing sentence** summarizes the main idea of the paragraph. It does not add any new details.	**Closing sentence** upgrades: • Add **transition words** • Introduce a **future thought** • Add an **encouragement to action** • Include a **question about the content** • Add a **personal opinion**

Paragraph Checklist

❏ Topic sentence

❏ 2-5 relevant details

❏ Closing sentence

❏ One or more transitions

❏ One or more other upgrades

❏ Spelling checked

❏ Grammar checked

Congratulations on finishing the workbook!

You now know everything you need to know to write strong paragraphs. Have fun being a paragraph expert!

Now it's time to check out the other workbooks in the series. Available in print & Kindle on Amazon.

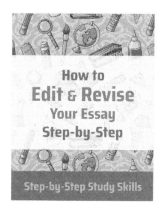

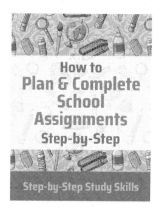

CERTIFICATE
OF
ACHIEVEMENT

THIS CERTIFICATE IS AWARDED TO

_____

IN RECOGNITION OF

_____

_____   _____

DATE   SIGNATURE

_____

TITLE

Made in the USA
Coppell, TX
24 September 2023

21940412R00052